You Can Miss Heaven Believing God Did Not Choose Women to Pastor

Such Belief Is Prejudice and Respect to Person

SIN Is SIN

If you have respect to persons, you commit sin, and are convinced of the law as transgressors.
James 2:9

Jennifer Pressley

FOREWORD

The language of the King James Bible, while beautiful and poetic, can also be a little challenging and obscure at times to those who are less familiar with the Bible or with this particular translation. One phrase that pops up quite a lot in this discussion is the concept of having "respect to persons."

At first glance it might seem as though this is talking about respecting people—having respect *for* persons. However, this is not the case. When James writes in **James 2:9** about having "respect to persons," he is referring to being prejudiced against certain persons or in favor of others. To "have respect to persons" means to be prejudiced or biased.

Contents

DEDICATION

I dedicate this book to the name of my Lord and Savior Jesus Christ, from whom all revelation and understanding comes.

I give honor to all of my church family, Breath of Life Ministries, who challenge me to teach them the truth so that they can stand on the truth of God's Word and not waver when they are asked: did God choose women to be pastors?

I dedicate this book to my husband, Ronnie Pressley, who has stood by my side and forever pushes me to be the best at what God has chosen me to do.

To my children, Leonard, Jazmin and her husband Tyrell, Ashley, and Gabrielle. Thank you for encouraging me and standing beside your mother.

To my brother Sidney, who was my first associate Pastor of Higher Praise. Thank you, my brother, for sharpening iron with me. I love you so much.

To my grandchildren, I hope this will enlighten your understanding in times of diversity and help you to seek God first and love truth so that you will always reap a harvest of peace and blessings. I love you all.

To my sister in Christ, Tonia Jennings—thank you for loving me and praying for me and searching out the scriptures with me and pushing me to get this book out to the public. You are a truly amazing woman of God.

INTRODUCTION

I remember, when I was nine years old, playing outside until dark. We heard loud music coming from the next street.

One night my sister, brother, and cousin decided to sneak over to the street where the music was coming from. To our surprise it was a small church packed with people singing, clapping, and shouting—but not only that. These people were young like us.

I was being raised Baptist and I did not know what this was, but I felt a power drawing me into that service. Next, onto my knees I went, in tears, mucus coming out of my nose. I was yelling, "Jesus, I thank you!"

The pastor took me home after the service was over, then told me that the revival was the following night. I never heard of a revival, but the next night I went back, and this time I was on my knees calling on Jesus's name, and words from God began to fill my mouth.

They said I was preaching for an hour on my knees. My sister and brother ran to get our mom so that she could witness this strange happening.

Mom came through the doors of that church. She fell on her knees beside me, but she would not touch me, because she knew that this was God, not her nine-year-old little girl who did not read the Bible like that.

I introduce you to a little girl who grew in her relationship with God and knowledge of his word and obedience to her pastors; God used me to heal people and cast out demons. Churches began to open their doors to me with a stipulation that I could not go into the pulpit. I had to preach from the floor. My head had to be covered. Next, I heard the bishop of one church tell them not to let me come into their pulpit because women were not allowed to speak from the pulpit. Well, this blew across my thoughts, because I wasn't a woman. I was only thirteen years old, so I figured they weren't talking about me. I was just ready for God to use me to heal, set free, and cast out devils.

The mother of that church came and positioned me on the floor in front of the pulpit and told me not to be too long, because their bishop didn't normally let women speak. Why did she say that? As soon as she gave me the microphone, God began to speak, and the power of God began to touch the people.

There were people falling on the floor giving their lives to God. Some were being healed. That bishop had said that he didn't let women speak because it went against God's law. God changed his mind.

That day I was wearing my hair in a ponytail; it was hanging and swinging all over the place. The Holy Spirit got into my ponytail and the bishop stood up, came up behind me, and grabbed my ponytail. He could not let go, because God was touching him as he was holding onto my hair; next, he fell onto the floor crying out to God.

After that, that bishop told everyone that God uses whoever he wants to use and that he was sorry. God will confirm his chosen ones no matter what age they are. That is why I am writing this book.

1. Did God make a law for women to be silent and not pastor?

God has really been speaking with me on the subject of women being chosen by God to pastor. This subject isn't new, but what we don't know about this subject will hurt us.

Over the years, when people have come to my church in Tennessee, some have said, "It's a curse to be under a woman pastor or to listen to a woman speak," and then walked out of our church.

The kids at our church continue to use God's word with their teachers and peers to defend being under a woman pastor. I hope you are blessed while reading and researching the statements in this book.

I hope you will write down the facts you discover about this truth. What I share in this book is not an opinion or a belief but a fact.

a. Understanding truth

If you really want truth, you belong to God, because the Holy Spirit is the Spirit of Truth. (**John 14:17**: "The spirit of truth, whom the world cannot receive, because it seeth him not.")

You have to understand this **truth**. If God did not want women to teach or pastor, he would have made this a *commandment* along with the Ten Commandments he gave to Moses. It would have read something like this: "Women are to keep silence and are prohibited from teaching, preaching, or pastoring in my name." **God has written no such law in his commandments** to be honored in his Holy Bible.

b. Eve and Adam transgressed verbal law

Eve transgressed the verbal law of God in the Garden of Eden by eating from the tree in the midst of the Garden. God had told her not to eat, but Eve did so anyway and gave the same food to her husband, Adam (**Genesis 3:3–7**).

c. Meaning of "your husband shall rule over you"

In **Genesis 3:13**, God said to the woman, "What have you done?" Then God talked to the snake, and then to Adam, and then he came to his conclusion in **Genesis 3:16**: The woman was punished with the pain of birthing a child, "and your husband shall have rule." (The word for "rule" in Hebrew means to "master" or "take advantage of.") Adam had failed to be strong and stand his ground with his beautiful wife, instead giving in to her words, so God told Eve that Adam would *master* her, or take advantage of her, meaning that **he would learn not to give in to his wife's cunning ways**—the domineering ways that had controlled him. This doesn't mean that he would *pastor* her, in the context of a church, nor was it about *putting a man in a certain position in the Church*. After all, Jesus said that he himself is the head of the Church (**Ephesians 5:23**).

d. The sin of disobedience reshaped relationships in this world

The sin of disobedience to God was committed in Adam and Eve's relationship, therefore *reshaping all relationships*, so *the people in them will desire domination of each other if they don't put Christ first.*

The issue with women pastoring isn't about men taking their *rightful place*, nor *a shortage of men pastoring*. The man is to be the head of the home, making sure his wife is protected and provided for. The wife is to make sure she meets the needs of her husband. This means that if he can't make the money to pay the bills alone, his wife should get a job and help; she is a helpmeet (**Genesis 2:20**).

Women pastoring is about God choosing shepherds after his own heart (**Jeremiah 3:15**).

Men have to learn not to give in to what's wrong when trying to please or keep their spouses. Choosing their wife when she is wrong, rather than standing for what's right, is choosing her over God. God puts in our hearts what is right and wrong. This also goes for women; don't choose your husband over God when he is wrong.

e. Root word of "silent"

God did not tell Eve to be *quiet*, which is what many people interpret from the word "silent." In the English language, *quiet* means to stop talking, and to be *silent* means to refrain from speaking or making a sound. The Hebrew word for silence is *nasb*, meaning *to take heed, to wait quietly, to be calm*. God was telling Eve to take heed of what her and Adam had done to all generations coming after them. God gave his command only for the positioning of the relationship.

f. God told Abraham to listen to his wife Sarah

In **Genesis 21:12**, God told Abraham to listen to whatever Sarah told him. Abraham took great care of Sarah, but God told Abraham, "Submit to your wife and I will honor you." **If God had wanted women to be silent**, quiet, only listening to and learning from their husbands, then **he would not have told Abraham to listen to whatever Sarah said about Hagar.**

In **2 Kings 22:14–20** and **2 Chronicles 34:22–28**, Huldah gave the kings a message from God: Disaster would strike the nation because they had forgotten God and worshiped idols. Huldah was married and was one of the seven prophetesses, the others being Sarah, Miriam, Deborah, Hanna, Abigail, and Esther.

This is also validated in the Old Testament scriptures that God used women in the position of prophetess, which is a messenger of God. She would warn the nation of Israel to stay away from idols before God utterly destroyed them.

2. JAMES 2:9, "TRANSGRESSOR OF THE LAW" MEANING

a. "Brethren" meaning in Hebrew

Nehemiah 6:14 mentions Prophetess Noadiah, a woman. **James 2:9** refers to a "transgressor of the law" as discussed in **Deuteronomy 1:16**: "And I charged your judges at that time, saying, Hear the causes between your brethren and judge righteously between every man and his brother and the stranger that is with him." The word for brethren in Hebrew is standard for a group of both men and women, so *brethren* here has no gender. The word here translated to English as "man" is the Hebrew *achim*, which also has no gender. If there were only one man and the rest of the group were women, this word would still be used, as it includes both sexes.

God disapproves of all partiality to persons. **Deuteronomy 1:17** says, "Ye shall not respect persons in judgement." This is another law from God:

Leviticus 19:15 says, "Thou shalt not respect the person of the poor nor honor the person of the mighty: but in righteousness shalt thou judge thy neighbor." Here again, the law in Leviticus says, "no respect to person of the poor or the mighty." What are we following? God's laws or the Pharisees' laws?

God said that this is a *command*. **To break a command is to transgress the law, which is the same as** *sinning*. As **James 2:10** states, "For whosoever shall keep the whole law and yet offend in one point, he is guilty of all."

b. Moses appoints judges

Moses appointed judges over tribes. The word translated into English as *judges* is *shaphat* in Hebrew and means ruler, shepherd, lawgiver, elder, or governor of God over tribes. In other words, a judge is a pastor (shepherd, governor, ruler, elder).

Moses's sister Miriam was a prophetess and elder (judge-pastor) over a portion of Moses's tribes. If Moses had gone against God's commandment in **Leviticus 19:15** not to have respect to person, he would have risked dying and going to hell.

Hebrews 13:17 commands, "Obey them that have Rule over you." This *rule* is different from what God told Eve. In **Hebrews 13:17**, *rule* means *to govern*—and *govern* means to direct, to control (as an action of men), to restrain, to keep in due *subjection*. It also refers to *administering the law* and maintaining superiority. In pastoring, to *rule* is, therefore, to take a leadership role. Pastors help keep your relationship with God pure by warning you, rebuking you, and giving truth.

c. Deborah, a judge and a military leader

Let's now look at **Judges 4:4–24**. There were no tabernacles back when Deborah would sit under the palm tree to judge God's people. Deborah was a pastor first, then a military leader asked by Barak to lead him in battle. She went with him but prophesied to him that the victory would come through another woman. Her prophecy came to pass.

You will find when studying the scriptures that God's word does not contradict itself. When you ask the Holy Spirit to give you an understanding to rightly divide the word of truth into its proper context, God will give you the facts about the culture of the time, including what was going on and why the people used the phrases they did. God gives us this aid so that we can understand and not have people missing out on Heaven because they don't understand the Jewish culture and the Hebrew language.

3. The Modern Definition of "hate" differs from the Hebrew

The meaning of the English term "hate" in the USA today is totally different from the Hebrew term based in Jewish culture, as you will see.

For example, **Malachi 1:2–3** and **Romans 9:13** state, "Yet I have loved Jacob, but Esau I have hated." Remember that Jacob was his mother's favorite and was the baby of the family; Esau was the eldest son and was favored by his father. Jacob's mother knew that Isaac was dying and that he was going to give everything to Esau because of tradition, but Jacob's mother told him to trick his father into thinking he was Esau, so he did.

When Esau came back and received nothing from his father, he was angry and hurt. So *why would God hate Esau* after knowing that Esau had received nothing and the rest of what he had—infertile land, which was his birthright— he gave to his brother for something to eat? Why would God *hate* him? Esau's people were the Edomites. Esau was angry with his father for giving away his blessing to his brother. Esau decided to disobey his father's wishes and marry outside of his covenant. Israel was a chosen nation, but the Edomites were a *heathen nation*. Marrying in the same family of the covenant God had established for Israel wasn't about keeping relationships inside your race or family but about keeping the people he had chosen for himself from being defiled through being introduced to idol gods. Why would God feel *hate* instead of *pity*?

An American dictionary definition (Merriam-Webster) says that hate is an extremely strong feeling of dislike, hostility, or enmity. To hate is to detest. These are all emotions. In Hebrew, however, the word translated into the English "hate" is *sane*, to separate yourself from someone. This definition does not involve being controlled by an emotion.

God separated his presence from Esau because Esau disobeyed his father and broke the covenant.

I hope you see from these examples that looking up the customs and language of that time is very important when studying God's word if you want to know the *truth* of God's word.

Why do we want to believe that God is prejudiced or has respect to person, or even that Jesus feels that a woman's place is in the home, seeing to her kids only, and that she has no place in God's eyes, nor a right to be whatever God wants her to be?

Our sinful nature will believe a *lie* before we believe the truth.

Jeremiah 3:15 says, "I will give you shepherds [the same word as that for *judges*] after my own heart."

God does not say that the shepherds will be after the heart of the pastor because they're his favorite niece or nephew or have a theology degree, but that God will choose his shepherds according to **1 Samuel 16:1–13**, "God told Samuel to go anoint Jesse's son with oil to be king."

Samuel went to Jesse's house and there were seven sons who passed by Samuel, but none of the seven was the chosen. Samuel asked Jesse if there was another son. Jesse said, "Yes, he is attending the sheep." David was called to stand before Samuel, and the Lord confirmed to Samuel that David was indeed the one God had chosen. God will always confirm his pastors and let you know it's him.

4. LET'S LOOK AT TWO SCRIPTURES: 1 CORINTHIANS 14:33 AND 2 CORINTHIANS 14:34-37

Let's look at two scriptures. The first is **1 Corinthians 14:33**. In this verse, Paul says, "God is not the author of confusion, but of peace, as in all the Church of the saints."

Now, the Corinthian Church was known for its divisiveness, for offering food up to idols, for litigation, for class divisions, and for respect to person, which is prejudice according to the Talmud of Orthodox Judaism.

Paul had a problem with members showing unity within the church in **1 Corinthians 1:10–12**, with some saying, "I am of Paul" and others saying they were of Apollos. **1 Corinthians 4:7** shows that Paul did not go along with having respect to person. Wanting answers, wanting to know who was trying to divide the Church, Paul asked, "For who maketh thee to differ from another?" In **1 Corinthians 4:14–15**, he said, "I write not to shame you, but as my beloved sons I warn you. For in Christ Jesus I have begotten you." In **1 Corinthians 4:17**, he continues, "For this cause have I sent Timothy, who is my beloved son, and faithful in the Lord. **Who shall bring you into remembrance of my ways, which be in Christ, as I teach everywhere in every church.**" **Acts 19:22** shows us that Timothy was under Paul's ministry.

Acts 18:2, 18–26 tell us that Priscilla and Aquila were commanded, along with all Jews, to depart from Rome. Priscilla was an evangelist and pastor along with her husband Aquila. Timothy and Titus were also taught by women.

Acts 17:34 states that "certain men cleaved unto Paul and believed," and a woman named Damaris also followed him.

Damaris was a female convert who listened to Paul's speech and gave her life to Jesus.

In **Acts 16:40**, Paul was released from prison, and afterwards he assembled the followers of Christ in the house of Lydia. Lydia took her name from her country. She was a businesswoman, and her business was selling purple dye and material. Purple was the most expensive color and was obtained from shellfish. The color was worn chiefly by princes and the rich. Lydia had a home or building large enough for Paul and his missionaries to stay in. She loved God and helped Paul with his ministry, pastoring the house church when Paul was in prison. **Lydia was a woman pastor.**

In **Romans 16:7**, Paul greets *Junia* and tells others that she is a kinswoman and fellow prisoner and that she is an apostle. What's more, **she was among the apostles who were in Christ *before him***.

So how can we think that Paul would go against women pastoring or teaching God's word? Such thinking contradicts God's word.

If Paul had been against women pastoring or teaching, he would never have told Timothy to remind his congregation of what Paul taught in every church. He had *no respect to person.*

Galatians 3:28 says, "There is neither Jew nor Gentile, slave nor free, male nor female." This was what Paul taught in all his churches.

5. CORINTHIANS 14:34

In **1 Corinthians 14:34**, Paul had to rebuke the Jews in the community because they were admitting the *laws of the scribes* (also known as Orthodox Judaism) into his church. *The laws of the scribes were not the written commandments of Moses* but were instead the traditions and ordinances of Orthodox Judaism, their man-made laws, which Jesus had corrected the scribes about. The scribes' man-made laws reflected their own hatred and disrespect for women in general, and especially for people who were poor and did not look like them. The people who believed in the Orthodox Jewish tradition and who converted to Christianity brought that man-made law into the Church for Christian women to abide by, and Paul was upset.

a. History of the law of the Pharisee

The history of the laws (and *roles of women*) in the Messianic Assembly may just *blow your mind*. Tim Hegg, author of the article "The Role of Women in the Messianic Assembly," says that the primary sources that inform us of the first-century through sixth-century culture of this group were the *Talmud* and the *Midrash* the legal writing of the Jewish nation. Early Judaism saw a woman's role as being centered around her home and family. Outside of the home and their roles within it, women were described by the Talmud as "lazy, stupid, vain, having a tendency for occult, and in many ways ... unteachable." According to Josephus, a Jewish historian, "woman ... is in all things inferior to a man." Women were not regarded as acceptable witnesses in a court of law.

Likewise, In Talmudic *halakha* (literature that deals with law and with the interpretation of the laws of the Hebrew scriptures), divorce is the right of the man only. The sphere of the woman was decidedly praised for childbearing, but women were considered on the same level as *Gentile slaves* or *dogs*.

For a woman to venture outside of her boundaries was frowned upon by the Talmud. The Talmud warned men against talking to women because women were seen as sexual snares for men. Women were encouraged to veil their faces outside of the home and not to look at men face to face or talk to men. Women were assumed to have a naturally uncontrollable sexual desire, and any time a woman was abused or raped, it was assumed *that she had seduced the man.* The Talmud suggested that a man could not withstand the seduction of a woman and was not responsible for any sexual advances he made upon her outside of her dwelling.

The Midrash states, "Let the words of the Torah rather be destroyed by fire than imparted to a woman." This meant that women could be taught the Torah only in relation to their duties, and a full teaching of the Torah should be reserved for men only. This is why, if they were to learn anything, women were to be taught by their husbands at home.

Now we can begin to get a little understanding of the background against which Paul had to correct any doctrine that was not from the *written commandment of God.*

b. Paul addresses spiritual gifts

First, Paul addressed *spiritual gifts* in
1 Corinthians 14:1–35.

Second, he addressed the *gift of tongues without an interpreter*, letting the Corinthians know that this gift didn't edify the Church. Instead, they were to prophesy, so that the Church could be edified or understand what God was saying to the Church.

Third, in **1 Corinthians 14:34–35**, Paul addressed the Corinthians allowing legalistic people, such as the Jews, to add to Paul's teaching the *oral law of the scribes*, which was not the *written law of Moses*. **Paul rebuked the Corinthians for saying, "And if they would learn anything, let them ask their husbands at home: for it is a shame in the church."**

Paul was outraged, essentially asking in **1 Corinthians 14:36**, in disbelief that someone would say such a thing in his presence, "What? Came the word of God out from you? Or came unto you only?" He was asking them, in all this foolishness and confusion, with the laws of men mixing with the laws of God, "Are you trying to tell me God is speaking through you and to others in this confusion?" Paul knew that this was not God. **God doesn't confuse us and mix the law of the scribes (the Talmud) with God's own written law**.

c. 1 Corinthians 14:37, "Things I write are the commandments of the Lord"

Fourth, Paul addressed what the Corinthians were to *do*: "Things that I write unto you are the commandments of the Lord" (**1 Corinthians 14:37**). They were *not* to do what is stated in **1 Corinthians 14:34–35**. Instead, he explained to them in **verse 40**, "Let everything be done decently and in order. This is what God is commanding you all to do." They were to show respect for each other's gifts and were not to take over the service just because they felt like they could.

Remember, in **1 Corinthians 14:34, women were told to keep silent; this was the order of the *law of the scribes*.** *God* never commanded women to keep silent. In **1 Corinthians 1:11**, Paul wrote, "It was declared unto me, by the household of Chloe ..." Who was Chloe? She was the head of her household and was *pastor over the home church*. She had to be important in the community for Paul to mention her name and to pay attention to her complaints concerning what was going on in the Church.

So, when we look at the Book of Acts, where Timothy was working under Paul's teachings to beware of these *false doctrines*, Paul was doing just what *a father of the Gospel* would do to keep his son on the *straight and narrow road of truth* while being surrounded by so much diversity.

6. What law was Paul going by?

Paul wrote in **1 Corinthians 6:12**, "All things are lawful unto me, but I will not be bought under the power of any." By this, he meant that the laws of the scribes were okay for those citizens who abided by them, *but Paul was not going to incorporate the laws of man* (the laws of the scribes) *into his Church.* **Paul went by the laws of God.**

What laws was Paul talking about when he mentioned the laws of God? He was referring to the laws of judging, the Mosaic law—Genesis, Exodus, Leviticus, Numbers, Deuteronomy, which is the true word of God—and the new testaments of Jesus Christ from Matthew, Mark, Luke, and John. Paul and the disciples went by the *Tanakh*, including the following passages:

> **Leviticus 19:15**: "Ye shall not do no unrighteousness in judgement: thou shalt not respect person."

> **Deuteronomy 1:16–18**: "God says, 'I charge your judges. Ye shall have no respect of person. I command you.'"

> **2 Chronicles 19:1–7**: "Jehoshaphat said to all the judges in the land, 'Take heed what ye do; for ye judge not for man, but for the Lord, who is with you in judgment. Wherefore now let the fear of the Lord be upon you; take heed and do it: for there is **no iniquity with the Lord our God, nor respect of persons, nor taking of gifts.**'"

> **Proverbs 24:23–25**: "These things also belong to the wise. It is not good to have respect of persons in judgment."

God makes no mistakes in whom he *chooses* to pastor his Church, but what has indeed happened is that a lot of women and men have not been *chosen by God* to pastor but have gone on their own theological degrees, greed for money, and disrespect of their leaders and put up their own buildings. People are missing Heaven because *pastors* and *preachers* refuse to study God's word thoroughly or they don't have the Holy Ghost to reveal the truth of scripture. This blood is on the hands of those pastors and Christians all over the world; everyone will be accountable for their own souls. This is not worth missing *Heaven* over.

2 Timothy 2:15 says, "Study to show yourself approved unto God, a workman that is not ashamed, rightly dividing the word of truth." Such study is *rightly dividing the word of truth*. We are *obligated* to perform this study, lest we become partakers of the sin of displaying respect of person (**Ephesians 5:7**). **This is sin. You can choose whether to receive this message or not.**

John 8:47 says, "He that is of God heareth God's words: ye therefore hear them not, because you are not of God." Truth sets us free from the bondage of sin. Respect to person is a *subtle sin* that has been around forever; it means we all have equal worth and should be treated unconditionally, without disrespect because of gender or status of any kind. **This sin can make you miss Heaven.**

Hosea 4:6 states, "My people are destroyed for lack of knowledge, also perish because they reject knowledge." Jesus Christ always admonished the women in his ministry. If Jesus had made a law against women pastoring, teaching, or carrying his message, **he would have told the Angel of the Lord to go to Peter or John, rather than the women, to tell the other disciples that he had risen.** Instead,

- "But he told Mary, go tell the others, he is not here" (**Matthew 28:6–7**).

- Jesus entrusted to a woman the testimony of his resurrection (**John 20:17**).

- Jesus considered the worth of a woman caught in adultery greater than the worth of the law of the Pharisees on the Sabbath (**Luke 13:16**).

- Jesus accepted women as disciples to travel with him in his ministry (**Luke 8:1–3**).

"God is not a man that he should lie" (**Numbers 23:19**). There is no prejudice in God. Prejudice is sin, and respect of person is sin, but **God has no sin in him**.

Ask yourself why someone wants Jesus Christ, who died for the sins of this world and gave us a choice to be forgiven of all our sins, to have sin in *him* by having prejudice against women being pastors, bishops, and apostles.

If Jesus Christ had prejudice against women teaching or pastoring, or against any race, ethnic group, or people of color, *our salvation would be null and void*. Jesus Christ is God, with *no sin*. God is perfect in all his ways. If you are a Christian and have prejudice against people of different races, people of color, women pastors, Spanish people, or Muslims, God is not in you and you are not a Christian. "Shall we continue in sin that grace may abound? Certainly not! How shall we who died to sin live any longer in sin?" (**Romans 6:1–4**). **Revelation 21:27** tells us that nothing *impure* will enter into heaven.

Jesus demonstrated his love and respect for women and his desire to bring the Jews into his order of true transformation with true deliverance from prejudice, unforgiveness, and respect of person through giving us his salvation. Jesus shows his disciples consistently that it's not about the place you come from, how rich you are, or what political party you belong to. Jesus crossed all barriers so that he could free those who are bound.

John 4:76 tells us that Jesus had a need to go to Samaria. Bear in mind that the Jews and Samaritans had no dealings with each other. Samaritans were considered Gentiles, even dogs, because they came about after the Assyrian captivity of the Northern Kingdom (721 BC). Jews could not talk to Samaritans, let alone share the gospel that was promised to the Jews first, but Jesus began to talk with the Samaritan woman at the well and told her that he was the living water. In this way, Jesus established for his disciples that prejudice was wrong.

Jesus told the Samaritan woman, "I give you living water that will never run out." His Holy Spirit is that living water that overflows in us to set free from prejudice those who are hurting, confused, or depressed. Jesus told the Samaritan woman, "There will come a time that they will not worship in the mountains, neither the Jews in Jerusalem, but the true worshippers will worship in *spirit* and in *truth*." How can you worship Jesus Christ in spirit and truth when you have a spirit of disobedience toward his commandment to have no respect of person (**Deuteronomy 1:17**)?

7. 1 TIMOTHY 2:9, "WOMEN, ADORN YOURSELVES"

In **1 Timothy 2:9**, Paul says to Timothy, "In like manner also women adorn themselves in modest apparel, no braided hair, pearls or costly jewelry." This indicates that they were teaching new converts how to dress. Paul was also letting the new converts know not to dress like the first-century Romans, where women would customarily braid or twist their hair high onto their heads, decorating the braids with jewels, gold adornments, and much more to get attention. Hairstyles were determined by social status, wealth, and profession. A woman's hairstyle expressed who she was and what her role in society was.

In **verse 10**, Paul is talking about new converts professing godliness even though they came from a background of being false teachers of the goddess Artemis and of being influenced by the cult of Artemis, in which female supremacy was the way of life and the women's dress was probably very seductive and provocative. These women needed to know how to dress and behave like Christians. Once again, this status of hairstyles made one have respect of person, while Paul advised against anything that would make a person feel like they were better than another. Instead, Paul taught how to dress in humility while maintaining confidence in who God created them be.

8. 1 Timothy 2:11–12, "Let the Women Learn in Silence"

While **verse 11** states that the women are to learn in silence with all subjection, the Greek phrasing means that they are to learn in stillness, in peace, and humble themselves. Again, these verses were coming into Christianity and teaching people how to behave as new Christians.

Again, **James 2:9** tells us, "If you have respect of person, You commit sin, and are convinced of the law as transgressors." Remember, a transgressor is one who disobeys and breaks the laws of God.

1 Timothy 2:11–12 says, "Let the woman learn in silence with all subjection. But I suffer not a woman to teach, nor to usurp authority over the man, but to be silent." Here, Timothy is being instructed by *Paul.* This is not Timothy talking, but most people think that it is. Paul wrote this to Timothy while Timothy was pastoring in Ephesus. Paul warned Timothy to guard against false doctrine and myths and to develop and mature in leadership. Paul instructs Timothy how to handle the women who are being taught how to carry themselves in business and as new converts to Christianity.

Ephesus was one of the largest cities in Asia Minor, with about 100,000 residents. Ephesus was known for its devotion to the goddess Diana, also known as Artemis to the Greeks. The income of many people in Ephesus revolved around Artemis-worship.

Acts 19:26–28 talks about Paul preaching about Jesus Christ and the people starting to believe and throw away their crafts and burn their curious arts and cultic books. These were valued at the equivalent of one million dollars. People in Ephesus blamed Christianity for threatening their business and culture.

Artemis was a fertility goddess thought to give and take life. She was called upon to speed the process of labor and ease labor pains. This cult was run entirely by women, and men played a subservient role.

Thus when Paul told Timothy that he would not permit "a woman to teach and usurp authority over the man" (**1 Timothy 2:12**), Paul was referring to the domineering women who were leaders and teachers in this all-female cult of Artemis that kept men subservient (as sex slaves) and those of other beliefs, such as Gnostics.

In 1 Timothy 2:11, which says, "Let the woman learn in silence," Paul was *not* talking about the female teachers, deacons, and pastors of his own ministry. Instead, he was talking about the women who were new converts to Christianity and were being taught how to carry themselves. Because some of these were women of authority who had abused their powers as teachers and leaders of the cult of Artemis, Paul told Timothy to let the women learn in *silence*—the Greek phrasing meaning *learn in peace*—because they were brutish, rude, and domineering. **He did *not* mean that they should be quiet.**

Once again, when **verse 11** states that the women are to learn in silence *with all subjection*, the Greek phrasing means that they are to learn in stillness, in peace, and humble themselves. Again, these verses were not talking about women of Paul's *clergy*, but women who were coming into Christianity and learning how to behave as new Christians.

Again, in **1 Timothy 2:12**, when Paul wrote to Timothy—not to the Church—"But I suffer not a woman to teach nor usurp," Paul was not talking about women of the clergy but about those women who were unlearned in the ways of Christianity and those from the Artemis cult. Here, the English word *usurp* is representing the Greek word *authentein*, meaning "abuse authority."

Many of these women who were under young Timothy's ministry were from an *all-female cult of a fertility goddess*, where they had been false teachers and taught and behaved in an abusive manner.

Paul was telling Timothy to teach these women that they were not to *abuse their authority* and overstep their boundaries but were to be in silence—again, in Greek, the word he used refers to *living in peace*, not to being quiet.

Remember, *Paul already had women pastoring and teaching in his ministry*, and *Timothy worked with those women*. (**1 Corinthians 16:19**: "Priscilla and Aquila salute you much in the Lord, with the church that is in their house.") Priscilla was a teacher, evangelist, and pastor along with her husband Aquila. They both shared the duties of the ministry.

a. 1 Timothy 2:13–14, "Adam first and not Eve": Gnosis and mythological beliefs

1 Timothy 2:13–14 says, "For Adam was first not Eve. Adam was not deceived but Eve." Here, Paul was addressing Timothy about the problem of *Gnostic* and mythological influences; Timothy was facing false teachings, such as Gnostic beliefs that Eve was a heroine because she desired a higher knowledge. (*Gnosis* means *knowledge*, and Gnosticism is a way of thinking that says that this world is horrible and the only way to save it is through a higher spiritual knowledge.) This mythology was designed to justify the fall of mankind due to Eve seeking knowledge from the snake in order to be like God.

These women dominating Ephesian culture with their influence and giving primacy to women over men had to come to an end.

1 Timothy 2:15 says, "Notwithstanding she shall be saved through childbearing." Paul knew that women were not saved through bearing children but that God saved *Eve*, with the punishment of pain while bringing forth children (**Genesis 3:16, 22**). Paul needed to put this in order for Timothy in **verse 15** because these women could get out of hand.

Genesis 3:16: "Unto the woman I will multiply thou sorrow and thy conception; in sorrow thou shalt bring forth children; and thou desire shall be for thy husband and he shall rule over you."

Genesis 3:22: "And the Lord God said, behold, the man is become as one of us to know good and evil and now, lest he put forth his hand and take also of the tree of life and eat and live forever."

God knew that outside of the Garden of Eden, both Adam and Eve would need to call on the name of the Lord and to live righteously before him in order to be saved.

Paul knew that in **Genesis 5:2**, God named Eve and Adam one name (Adam). God was showing humankind the oneness of these two human beings right from the beginning.

If Paul had been talking here against women pastoring or teaching, he would have been doing as the Pharisees had done, and the word of God would be of *no effect*, as Paul made clear to the Corinthians:

- **1 Corinthians 11:1**: "Be ye followers of Christ as he is."

- **1 Corinthians 11:10**: "The woman ought to have power on her head because of the angels." (Notice that this says "angels," not "man" or "her husband.") Jewish traditions regarded angels as protectors of God's glory and honor.

- **1 Corinthians 11:11–12, 16**: "Neither is the man without the woman, neither is the woman without the man, in the Lord. For as the woman is of the man, so is the man of the woman. But all things are of God."

- "If any man seems to be contentious [to dispute this], we have no such custom, neither the churches of God."

b. God refers to both Adam and Eve as one humankind

In **Genesis 5:2**, God referred to both Adam and Eve together as *Adam*, meaning *humankind*, with no gender. **Genesis 4:1** says, "Adam knew his wife Eve; she conceived and bore Cain, and said, 'I have gotten a man from the Lord.'" "Man" here means *mankind*.

Why is this important? It shows that God did not need an extended vocabulary to say what he meant, because he put those words in the hearts of his people. The only creatures Eve had seen who looked like her and her husband were herself and Adam; she knew that her baby did not look like an animal, so she called him *mankind*. After this, God give them wisdom to distinguish between male and female.

c. Qualification of deacons, bishops, elders

If we read **1 Timothy 3:8–13**, especially **verse 10**, we see that qualification as a deacon *wasn't geared to only the male gender*. Women, such as Phoebe and a few other women, were also called deacons (the Greek word *diakonos* translates as *servant*—"deaconess" or laborers, helpers). Women elders, pastors, and bishops, including

Phoebe and Priscilla, were not left out; Priscilla taught as a pastor with her husband in their ministry and home church. *This passage was not addressing only men.* Why? To address only men would show *respect to person.*

Remember, in Hebrew and other Semitic languages, it is standard for a group of men and women to be referred to by a masculine noun or pronoun. This means that if there is only one man in the group and the rest are women, the masculine word is used to include both sexes.

Women are not excluded from being qualified as deacons and bishops. This passage sets the order that bishops and deacons can be married only once: A male bishop should have only one wife, and a female bishop should have only one husband. Likewise, a male deacon should have only one wife, and a female deacon should have only one husband.

You can't say, "I am a Christian and I don't have to accept God's words," following only the parts you like. If you do this, you are not following Christ.

Dorcas was a deaconess and she was pastor over Paul's churches while he was in jail. She took care of all the affairs of the churches at that time.

d. Timothy, behave yourself

In **1 Timothy 3:15**, we can tell that Timothy was being trained by Paul to be a pastor. Paul tells Timothy that if he tarried long, Timothy "mayest know how to behave yourself in the house of the Lord." Timothy was young, and Paul told him, "Let no man despise your youth, but be the example of the believers in word, conversation, in charity, in spirit. Give attendance to reading, to exhortation, *to doctrine* (**1 Timothy 4:12–13**).

Remember, the whole Bible is *doctrine*. You can't exclude any of the books or passages of God's word, picking out only what you want.

In **1 Timothy 4:16**, Paul lets Timothy know that there is no shortcut: "In doing this; you will save thy self and them that hear."

1 Peter 3:15 states, "But in your hearts sanctify Christ as Lord. Make him your master, ruler. Always be prepared to give an answer for the hope that's in you." This means that we are to set Christ (the one appointed as Lord) as our leader.

Paul wrote in **1 Timothy 5:21**, "I charge thee before God, and the Lord Jesus Christ, and the elect angels, that thou observe these things without preferring one before the other, doing nothing by partiality." Notice here the phrase *doing nothing by partiality*. This should tell you that **Paul had *no* respect of person**.

To choose a man to be a pastor rather than to obey God, *who chooses his pastors after his own heart*, is a dangerous thing. God should always guide pastors and bishops to appoint those men or women who have been obedient under their leadership, as well as faithful; the bishops and pastors need to know the works of those they appoint. The pastor will lay hands on that man or woman and give him or her the approval from God to operate with their gifts under that ministry.

9. "YE DO ERR"

1 Thessalonians 5:12–13 states, "Know them which labor among you and are over you in the Lord, and admonish you."

How can I, as a pastor, make a person coming from another church into a youth pastor, deacon, or minister without knowing them? For all I know, that person could have been disobedient at the other church and tried to turn members against that pastor. I would need to call the last church that person left, then see if the person can sit and be obedient to leadership—following orders, being a janitor, maybe. I need to see how the person takes correction and operates in a position of humility. I need to *know* the person whom I feel the Lord is placing over his people in a position of authority.

I remember when a church hired a youth leader without consulting God through prayer and fasting because his résumé looked good. Little did they know that a year down the road he would not believe in Jesus Christ, although he could quote scriptures from the Bible. This person did not have the Holy Spirit, but he could tolerate any kind of environment in order to get his desires met. This person finally started doing what he does best—lewd acts with the kids. He looked the part of a leader and acted the part of a leader, but he wasn't a leader from God. Seeking God first and coming to know that woman or man is not the act of partiality but the result of listening to the word of the Lord—**1 Thessalonians 5:12–13**, "know them that labor among you."

When Paul wrote in **1 Timothy 5:21**, "I charge thee before God, and the Lord Jesus Christ and the elect angels," he was letting Timothy know that he was giving a *direct command* and should *not* be taken lightly.

When we take certain books of the Bible as being true for today but take some scriptures as not applying to today, we need to study carefully to see if those scriptures were indeed fulfilled by Jesus Christ so that we can know that we don't need to obey them in this generation, or else we will act in the *spirit of deception*.

If you don't know how to study God's word, don't just go along with every wind of doctrine you hear because it is spoken by well-known bishops or rich pastors. Fame and wealth don't mean that these people are speaking the truth. Instead, if you don't understand, *ask God to give you understanding*. He will. Look for a good church that teaches the truth of the scriptures along with facts about history and culture.

This is more than just God using whoever he wants. God spoke through a donkey to save Balaam from the angel of the Lord that could have killed him (**Numbers 22:22–30**). God used a woman to tell Peter and the others that he was risen. God used his prophetess Anna to tell the good news of the baby Jesus being the Messiah to those looking for the Messiah (**Luke 2:36**).

This is Jesus Christ saying, "I am coming for my people one day, and this message has to go out to my people who don't have an understanding that respect to person is a *sin*, and this sin will keep them out of Heaven." God wants you to know that he commands us not to have respect to person—and not only those people he uses to speak through. **Remember the message**: God is trying to get our garments as white as snow before we die, and if this ungodly belief is hindering you from going to Heaven, then God is speaking to you to let you know that it's not right to disobey his commandment.

James 2:10: "Whoever keeps the whole law but stumbles at just one point is guilty of breaking it all."

Don't let anyone tell you that God doesn't mean that you will miss Heaven if you keep breaking one of his laws. *You will miss Heaven.* **Total obedience is key to having a relationship with God and ensuring you will make it to Heaven.**

Before God comes for us, he exhausts every effort to make sure we learn the truth, and he gives us time to accept the truth and repent of our sins. **"Repent for studying his word in error" (Matthew 22:29).**

In **Matthew 22:29** Jesus told the Sadducees, "Ye do err, not knowing the scriptures, nor the power of God." Could this be you? This was me at one time. I thank God for giving me the love to know the truth, no matter how much it hurts me to admit I was wrong.

You can believe that God can use women to pastor but choose to be under a male pastor. Preference isn't a sin, but being convinced that God does not choose women to pastor and allowing your actions to display rejection of female ministers is directly disobeying the law of God.

10. TITUS WAS A GENTILE

Titus was a Gentile. Paul wrote to him to instruct him, encourage him, and help him organize the Church. Titus and Timothy were very young, and Paul said that leaders in the Church not only should know the word of God but should also live their lives in a style that reflects God's character, maintaining their homes, children, and wives and husbands. He included *women as well as men* in leadership positions.

Titus had to deal with those who were professors of religion. He had to prove himself to be a teacher for them so that they would treat him with respect.

Paul wrote to Titus, calling him "mine own son after the common faith" (**Titus 1:4**): "For this cause left I thee in Crete, that thou shouldest set in order the things that are wanting, and ordain elders in every city, as I had appointed thee" (**Titus 1:5**).

Phoebe was not left out. She helped Timothy and Titus order their ministry. *Lydia also wasn't left out.* She helped to set in order the ministries that needed help. *Priscilla and Aquila were not left out.* They also helped set in order the ministries that needed help.

In **1 Titus 1:9–12**, Paul wrote, "Holding fast the faithful word as he hath been taught that he may be able by *sound doctrine both to exhort and to convince the gainsayers.* For there are many unruly and vain talkers and deceivers, *especially of the circumcision* whose mouth must be stopped, teaching things they ought not, for filthy lucre's sake. One of them even a prophet of their own, said 'The Cretians [Cretans] are always liars, evil beast, slow bellies.'" Cretans had a notorious reputation for lack of moral integrity in 600 BC. Paul says, "This witness is true, wherefore rebuke the Cretians sharply, that they may be sound in the faith, not giving in to Jewish fables, and commandments of men, that turn from the truth" (**Titus 1:13–14**). Here, Paul let Titus know that they were not to follow the commandments of men—*the oral laws of the Pharisees, Jews, and scribes.*

You can't let anyone turn you away from the truth. The devil and people who are deceivers will try to tell you that this book is not true, but look at the facts for yourself and study it with your Bible, and God will open your eyes to the truth. Look at the following verses:

> **Romans 16:1–23**: "Paul extended greetings to all women and men" (no respect to person).

> **Titus 2:1–4**: "But these are the things which become sound doctrine. That the aged men [gender is mentioned here] be sober, grave, temperate, sound in faith, in charity, in patience. The aged women likewise, that they be in behavior as becometh holiness, not false accusers, not given much wine [this doesn't refer to alcohol, but to grape juice that has sat at room temperature but not fermented], *teachers* of good things. That they may teach the young women to be sober, to love their husbands, to love their children."

We can see in **Titus 2:1–4** that even women who were not evangelists, pastors, deacons, or elders were still given the privilege of teaching. Titus and Paul were never against women being teachers or pastors. Paul never went against women; he let God use them in the service of worshiping God.

11. ORAL LAW OF THE JEWS

The oral law of the Jews, later written down and called the *Talmud*, was the *interpretation* of Moses's law by the scribes and Pharisees. The Talmud is followed by Orthodox Jews today, and they consider it to have equal authority with the Bible.

The scribes and Pharisees falsely claimed that the oral law had been passed down by word of mouth from Moses. This was why the Pharisees wanted to kill Jesus and Jesus went against the Pharisees; Jesus rejected their man-made laws and legalistic spirit, as did Paul.

"Then came to Jesus Scribes and Pharisees, which were of Jerusalem, asking why do thy disciples transgress the tradition of the elders?" (**Matthew 15:1–2**). Who were the elders? Pharisees. Some people believed that in the time of Ezra, God gave Moses something more than the law, *but the Pharisees added their own traditions to the law of God.*

12. The Pharisees made their laws more important than God's

Mark 7:1–3 says, "Then came the Pharisees and certain Scribes unto Jesus. When they saw some of his disciples eat bread with unwashed hands they found fault. For the Pharisees, and all the Jews, except they wash their hands oft eat not, holding the tradition of the elders." We can see in these verses how the Pharisees' oral (man-made) law is different.

13. Jesus always refers back to the written law of Moses

In **Mark 7:5**, the Pharisees and scribes asked Jesus, "Why walk not thy disciples according to the tradition of the elders, but eat bread with unwashed hands?" to which Jesus responded, "Well Isaiah prophesied of *you* hypocrites, *as it is written*, these people honor me with their lips, but their heart is far from me. In vain do they worship me. *Laying aside the commandment of God*, ye hold *the tradition of men, as the washing of pots and cups* but reject the commandment of God" (**Mark 7:5–9**). In quoting Isaiah, Jesus referred to the written (Mosaic) law, drawing attention to the fact that the Pharisees were disregarding the written law for their own traditions. In **verses 10–23**, Jesus let them know that they were bringing Jewish religious practices into conflict with the far older commandments of the Old Testament. In other words, he was telling the Pharisees that they were hypocrites.

In **Matthew 15:3–6**, Jesus calls attention to *written scripture*, asking, "Why do you also *transgress the commandment of God by your tradition*? For God commanded, saying, Honor thy father and mother: and, He that curseth father or mother let him die the death. But you say, Whosoever shall say to his father or mother, It is a gift [a dedication to the temple] by whatsoever thou mightest *profit by me*." When Jesus said "thou mightest profit by me," he meant receiving a monetary donation; that was how they would profit—by making people believe that their money was being given to the temple when really it went into their pockets for their selfish gain. Jesus goes on to say, "and honor not his father or mother, he shall be free. *Thus have ye made the commandment of God of no effect by your tradition*."

In **Matthew 15:12**, the Pharisees were offended after hearing the truth. Jesus had put them on the spot, because the people did not know the truth about the laws they were following—did not know which were the laws of God and which were the laws of the Pharisees. The people thought they were following the laws of God, not knowing that the laws of the Pharisees were being imposed on them too.

The Pharisees made their laws more important than God's commandments. Jesus was bringing the truth to set free the people who were blind. Jesus does the same today. Pastors are not teaching the whole truth, only the truth that justifies their beliefs for their organizations. God requires us to study his word, find the truth, and get away from the tradition and religion of man, because **the doctrines of our organizations are contrary to God's word**.

We see in **Matthew 12:1–14** that once again Jesus kept the Pharisees in check by reminding them that they had no right to create *extra burdens of traditions with observances that were not laid down in the Mosiac law*. In **verse 3**, Jesus took them back to the *written scriptures* about David in **1 Samuel 21:1–6**:

> **Matthew 12:** "At that time Jesus went on the Sabbath day through the corn and his disciples were hungry and began to pluck the ears of corn, and to eat.
>
> 2 "But when the Pharisees saw it, they said unto him, Behold, thy disciples do that, *which is not lawful* to do upon the Sabbath day.
>
> 3 "But he said unto them, ***Have ye not read what David did***, when he was an hungered, and they that were with him.

4 "How he *entered into the house of God, and did eat the showbread, which was not lawful for him to eat, but only for the priests.*

"Or did you read how the priests profaned in the temple [*profaned* meaning 'to treat as communion'] *the Sabbath, and are blameless*?

"But Jesus said unto them *that he is greater than the temple.*

"But if ye had known what this meaneth, I will have mercy, and not sacrifice, *ye would not have condemned the guiltless.*

"*The son of man is Lord of the Sabbath.*"

The Pharisees were always looking to kill Jesus because of something he was saying, **but they did not realize that he was the creator of the world walking in flesh**. In **Matthew 12:9**, Jesus went to the synagogue, and in the following verses, he continued to keep the Pharisees in check:

"There was a man that had a withered hand. They asked him if it was *lawful* to *heal on the Sabbath day, that they might accuse him.*

"Jesus answered them, 'What man shall have one sheep, and if it falls into the pit on the Sabbath day will he not lift it out?'

"Jesus asked, 'How much is the life of a man better than a sheep?'"

Here, Jesus was basically asking, "Is it lawful to do good on the Sabbath?" In **verses 13 and 14**, Jesus told the man to stretch forth his hand and be healed, and then the Pharisees went out and held a council against Jesus to destroy him.

These were examples that Paul followed in teaching and in his churches, according to the written (Mosaic) law. These were the only laws for everyone to go by, including Paul and others following Jesus Christ. The Old Testament included more than 600 laws, along with prophecies by prophets Daniel, Joel, Jeremiah, Isaiah, and many more. These were the same laws that Jesus referred to, and he let the world know that he had fulfilled certain laws of the written law of Moses, *so we don't have to observe those laws in the same way they were observed in the Old Testament.*

For example, Jesus Christ fulfilled the law concerning the Sabbath, so we don't have to go to church on a Saturday or esteem one day more than another, because *he is Lord of the Sabbath* (**Matthew 12:8**; **Romans 14:5**). We don't have to kill rams or lambs for sacrifices anymore because Jesus fulfilled the need to sacrifice by going on the cross and becoming that sacrifice for us (**Hebrews 10:1–18**; **Malachi 3:6–15**).

Whenever you read the word of God, remember this: Jesus and his disciples always referred back to the written law of Moses, "for it is written, saith the Lord" (*not* "says the law" or "it is lawful" or "traditions of the elders," because that would mean the laws of the Pharisees). In the Bible, if God is talking or if Paul or the disciples are talking about the commandments that the people of God should follow, the text will always refer to the *written law of scripture*. But if the *oral law* of the Pharisees is being discussed, the text will start with "says the law" or it will follow it up with a judgment of the thing in question, such as "Why do you transgress the laws of the elders?"—which is also called "the traditions of the elders"—but never with "God said" or "the prophet said" (**Romans 14:11**).

This is how you can know if the Bible is discussing the oral law of the Pharisees. The oral law will always introduce you to a conversation about keeping the laws of the traditions of the elders. The written law will not.

I hope you understand that this is neither an opinion nor my thoughts on this matter but *God's word*. Thank God for the facts of history revealing the truth that will make us free!

Take this seriously. When God commands us to do something and we don't follow through on his commandment, *we have transgressed the law.* **Transgression is a sin** committed when we do not obey God's commandment, and *this sin can send us to hell.* This sin is just like the sins of adultery, lying, fornication, gossip, pride, unforgiveness, and anger. If you don't repent and get rid of these sins, **you will not make it to Heaven.**

This prejudice—respect to person—is a sin. It doesn't matter what you believe; belief is not based on facts, so it's not valid to live according to it. God's word is valid, and everything in the Bible is backed up by the facts of history about the culture in which it was written.

14. The law Paul went by

This is the law of God, which Paul went by. Remember, there are three phrases that are used: "saith the law" (**1 Corinthians 14:34**), "the laws of the elders and tradition of the elders" (**Mark 7:5**), which indicate the law of the Pharisees, and "it is written," which indicates God's law (Mosaic law) and which is backed up by Holy Scripture.

The Old Testament (the law of Moses) is usually referred to in the New Testament with the phrase "it is written." For example, **1 Corinthians 1:19** says, "For it is written, I will destroy the wisdom of the wise," referring to what God said in **Isaiah 29:14**, "for the wisdom of their wise men shall perish, and the understanding of their prudent men shall be hid."

1. In **1 Corinthians 1:31**, we see another example: "That, according as it is written, he that glorieth, let him glory in the Lord." Here, "written" means it was *spoken by God to Moses.*

2. **Jeremiah 9:23**, "Thus saith the Lord, let not the wise man glory in his wisdom."

3. In **1 Corinthians 1:19**, Paul wrote, "For it is written I will destroy this wisdom of the wise." This verse is referring to the *written word* recording the words from the mouth of God to Isaiah (**29:14**), "for the wisdom of the wise men shall perish, and the understanding of the prudent men shall be hid."

    Paul wrote in **Romans 4:16**: "but to that also which is of the faith of Abraham; who is the father of us all, as it is written, *I have made thee a father of many nations.*"

Genesis 17:5: "Neither shall thy name any more be called Abram, but thy name shall be Abraham; for a father of many nations have I made thee."

Galatians 4:27: "For it is written, rejoice, thou barren that bearest not; break forth and cry, thou that travailest not: for desolate hath many more children than she which hath a husband."

Isaiah 54:1: "Sing, O barren, thou that didst not bear; break forth into singing, and cry aloud, thou that didst not travail with child: for more are the children of the desolate than the children of the married wife, saith the Lord."

1 Peter 1:16: "Because it is written, be ye holy; for I am holy."

Leviticus 11:44: "For I am the Lord your God: ye shall therefore sanctify yourselves, and ye shall be holy; for I am holy."

Here are a few more examples:

- **1 Corinthians 9:9**: "For it is written in the law of Moses, thou shalt not muzzle the mouth of the ox that treadeth out the corn." (**Deuteronomy 25:4**: "Thou shalt not muzzle the ox when treading out the corn.")

- **1 Corinthians 14:21**: "In the law it is written, with men of other tongues will I speak to this people." (**Isaiah 28:11**: "For stammering lips and another tongue will he speak to his people.")

- **1 Corinthians 15:45–51**: "And so it is written the first man Adam was made a living soul." (**Genesis 2:7**: "And the Lord God formed man of the dust of the ground, and breathed into his nostrils the breath of life; and man became a living soul.") Notice that Jesus and Paul and the rest of the apostles always refer back to the Mosiac law or the prophets of the Bible to establish foundational truth.

Paul always let his churches know when the Lord was commanding or saying something rather than him.

For example, in **1 Corinthians 7:10**, Paul wrote, "unto the married I command, not I, but the Lord."

When Paul is sharing his instruction, not the instruction of the Lord, he makes that clear, as in **1 Corinthians 7:12**, "But to the rest speak I, not the Lord." Paul had a *fear of God* that made him avoid playing with the possibility of losing his soul to hell. It's sad that some pastors are filled with pride and can't say that they are wrong, going to hell rather than getting it right. Don't let that be you.

Paul also wrote in **1 Corinthians 7:6**, "I speak this by permission, and not of commandment," meaning that he was not quoting God's written scripture. **Paul did not partake of sin at any level,** after his eyes was blinded by God on the road of Damascus; he committed to living a sinless life.

In **Philippians 3:1–21**, Paul warned the Philippians to beware of dogs, meaning Judaizers. These were Jews who professed to be Christians. Even today, Judaizers believe that the law of circumcision is the way to salvation. Paul knew the beliefs of the Judaizers all too well, because those were his beliefs before he was born again as a Christian. In **Philippians 3:5**, he uses the phrase "Hebrew to Hebrew," meaning being a true-blooded pure Jew. Paul had been a Pharisee; an Orthodox defender, observer, and expounder of the Old Testament; and a student of the great teacher Gamaliel (**Acts 22:3**).

In **Philippians 3:6**, Paul wrote of persecuting the Church; he had been zealous about Judaism, so he had persecuted the Church to get rid of Christianity and Jesus Christ. In **verse 8**, Paul wrote that he viewed all his previous credentials as loss, or *dung*, basically saying, "I don't care about what I attained through education and earthly gains and Jewish privileges," including those of the Sanhedrin council. Paul knew that he wanted to be totally immersed in Christianity. He wanted to humble himself and get rid of all his pride so that he could *win Christ*, meaning make Jesus his savior and Lord. Paul, being an expert in the law of the Pharisees and the scribes, knew that Judaizers were implementing their laws in his churches. Paul was not going to compromise his Christianity because of what he had been a part of before. He had rid himself of all those false beliefs, rituals, and man-made laws. Paul walked in like mind with all the disciples of Jesus Christ and Christ's teachings. The disciples of Jesus Christ were not divided on the teachings of Jesus Christ as they went forth to establish churches all across Asia Minor and the rest of the world.

Jesus Christ let his followers know that they were not to follow the law of the Pharisees because the Pharisees were hypocrites. Jesus taught that **when we follow after him, there will be no division concerning his teachings**.

In **Luke 11:37–54**, Jesus called out the Pharisee who became upset with him for healing the woman on the Sabbath. The Pharisees wanted to catch him saying something wrong so that they could kill him. But Jesus knew every thought. In **verses 39–43**, Jesus said to the Pharisees, "You rather clean your cups and plates on the outside and leave the inside of your hearts full of ravening and wickedness. Ye fools! You rather give alms of such things ye have, you say this is clean unto you. Woe unto you, Pharisees, ye love the uppermost seats in the synagogues, and greetings in the market. Woe unto you Scribes and Pharisees, hypocrites! For ye are graves which appear not, and the men that walk over them are not aware of them." Jesus let everyone know that the Pharisees and scribes had a form of godliness but denied the power of God.

If you study the scriptures from Matthew to Revelation, you will see that each book that the apostles wrote was written under the leadership of the Holy Ghost. Each apostle wrote about what happened in his presence, and the other apostles wrote a little more, adding to what the others did not put in their books, and another apostle summed them up. These books, mixed with some Old Testament prophecies, will give you the ability to research the time, place, and culture to understand the facts and the *truth*.

Reading the King James version of the Bible, you will never see anything in God's word showing the apostles following their own beliefs based on Christ's teachings and leading the people of God astray. Why do we find ourselves making up our own doctrines for various denominations and organizations? This is the sin of pride and self-glory, the sin of not believing the total truth of God's word.

That's why there is so much confusion.

15. THE DIFFERENCE BETWEEN BELIEF AND THE TRUTH

Most people believe whatever they want to believe, whether their belief is right or wrong, or whatever feels right to them. In this case, what you don't know will hurt you and send you to hell, because not following God's law is a sin. **Revelation 21:27** says that no sinner will enter into heaven.

Song of Solomon 2:15 says that it is the little foxes that destroy the vine. When you doubt the truth and don't want to hear the truth because of what you were taught to believe, however, this can be a little fox that will keep us from entering the Kingdom of Heaven.

Remember, belief in something doesn't make that thing right, because belief is not based on truth. Truth is based on facts that are present and tangible before one's eyes and that can be proven. **2 Timothy 3:16–17**: "All scripture is given by inspiration of God, and is profitable for doctrine, for reproof, for correction, for instruction in righteousness. That the man of God may be perfect, thoroughly furnished unto all good works." The word of God needs no explanation, only research about the language in which it was written and about proper interpretation of that language, so that we love God and, growing in our relationship with Christ, don't misunderstand what the apostles meant as they were used by God to write the Holy Bible. The Bible is God talking.

Some say the Bible was written too many times. I say I am glad it was written in my language, because I can't read Hebrew or Greek or Arabic or Italian. The Bible being written so many times doesn't mean that it contradicts, misleads, confuses, or lies. God's word has the power to cast out demons, heal the sick, and transform a sick mind. Those who try to read the Bible like an ordinary book will find themselves confused and say it is contradictory and misleading, because you cannot read God's word without the Holy Spirit inside you, helping you understand or giving you an understanding. Neither can you interpret the Holy Bible with your own opinions.

"Knowing this first, no prophecy of the scripture is of any private interpretation. For the prophecy came not in old time by the will of man: but holy men of God spoke as they were moved by the Holy Ghost" (**2 Peter 1:20–21**). The word of God says that scripture is not given to any person's interpretation but is understood through revelation that comes from God backed by facts of history and culture.

Opinions have no room for God's word, but revelation from God brings forth facts that bring forth truth, and truth sets us free. If you are a pastor, deacon, or minister, you should want to be teachable, humble, patient, loyal, and committed to God. If you are under a leader who is teaching the word of God by showing facts that are backed up by the word of God, you can't argue with that teaching, because it is truth. The only reason someone will argue with the truth is because that person is *prideful*. **Proverbs 16:18** tells us, "Pride goes before destruction, a haughty spirit before a fall," and **1 Corinthians 2:10** says, "But God revealed them unto us by his spirit. For the spirit searches all things, yea, the deep things of God."

I want to study and search the deep things of God and learn everything I need to know to be more like him and to understand who he is, how I can be his servant, who the devil's servants are, how I can see the devil when he is dressed like a saint, what I need to do to maintain my Christian lifestyle, and how to know whether someone is preaching the truth or a lie.

When you study God's word, go to Bible study, ask questions in Bible study, study your Bible at home, obey your spiritual leaders, ask God to give you the love to pray and do what's right, and are consistent with attending your church, then you will find yourself loving God more and tearing down those things in your life that make you go against God's word because you feel that he doesn't mind or care. Well, God cares about you enough to let you know that you will have to be perfect as the Father in Heaven is perfect (**Matthew 5:48**), that he might present to himself a glorious Church (**Ephesians 5:27**) that should be holy and without blemish, and that no spot or blemish will enter into the Kingdom of Heaven.

So if your pastor tells you that God knows your heart and understands that you still have prejudice against people—people of color or white people or Muslims or mixed-race marriages or people who look different from you—that you use profanity, that you get angry until you have thoughts of beating or killing someone, that you desire to see harm come to someone who did you wrong, that you think your bad attitude toward others because of hurt from past relationships or family gives you an excuse to treat and talk to people awfully, that you can't forgive people, and that you drink wine or beer, and your pastor says, "That won't stop you from going to Heaven," you should be aware that all of these things will stop you from going to Heaven.

Everyone wants redemption according to how they think they should have it. Everyone loves to say, "I am a Christian," but they don't always like going to church. If you don't like to spend time with Jesus and with the saints of God like Jesus asks us to do, you don't love Jesus or have the Holy Spirit. The Church is not the building; the Church is Jesus living in your life and giving you a love for him that will draw you to joining a church that is controlled by the Holy Spirit and that will cause you to want to become subject or submissive to the authority of the man or woman of God so that you can learn to humble yourself, to follow and hear God, and learn of God through your spiritual leader.

The Holy Spirit will judge and find you guilty when you are wrong. So many people have the savior but have not received the fullness of Jesus Christ, which is the Holy Spirit. We don't want to feel guilty or bad about the wrongs we do to ourselves and everyone else, including Jesus Christ. That is why Jesus left us grace—not so that we can abuse grace, but so that we understand that if we do fall once or twice, we should *repent* and ask God to forgive us. In that case, he is compassionate and will forgive our sins. But if you ask God to forgive you and then in the next hour you sin, ask Jesus to forgive you again, and then sin again and again, you might as well not ask Jesus to forgive you, because grace doesn't work like that. Jesus already knows your heart, and once saved is not always saved: "And who have fallen away to be brought back to repentance, seeing they have crucified to themselves the son of God afresh, and put him to an open shame" (**Hebrews 6:6**).

16. ONCE SAVED, NOT ALWAYS SAVED

The belief that once saved is always saved is being preached to many people, but it is not true. The Bible gives us truth. The truth is that you need to repent and make up your mind to live right. It's not hard when you've left your old ways behind. Living this Christian life, the way God intended for us to live from the beginning, is a wonderful experience of true living. Jesus is soon to come, and time is winding down. Jesus knows that if you are truly a Christian, you want to put away your selfish deeds and say, "Lord Jesus, I need you to come into my life and forgive me of all my sins, and I believe you died on the cross and rose again on the third day, and you went to hell in my place. Save me and fill me with your Holy Spirit, and give me a hunger and a thirst for your word and for prayer and fasting. Humble me and help me to love to go to church and be a part of the family of God so that I can grow and be strengthened and understand your word. Help me to take off the negative way of thinking and put on the new positive way of thinking, and if there is any prejudice in me of any kind, remove it, Lord. I thank you for a new heart, a new way of thinking, and a new understanding of your word. I want more of you, Lord, and less of me. Here I am, Lord. This is it."

Please get your Bible and search all the scriptures, look for information on the culture and language of the time, and let God open your understanding of Holy Scripture so that you won't be left out of the Kingdom of Heaven. Salvation is through the truth of the word of God and the facts of scripture.

I thank God that he didn't let me be satisfied with knowing that he can speak through a donkey. God revealed through his word that it's just not about him being the creator of all things, being able to give an animal a voice to speak, but about him revealing the truth to deliver his people from the lies of false teachings. Some of us have become entangled in the snare of sin because certain information was not available in earlier times, but it is available now to set us free from sin and error. I feel like jumping, running, and giving God praise for his knowledge, wisdom, and understanding.

I'm glad I wasn't satisfied with knowing that God used a woman to first carry his word to the disciples.

I am glad I was not satisfied with knowing that God made woman and man to coexist.

I'm glad God revealed to me the real importance of this message about women pastoring. He doesn't want me to commit the sin of prejudice, respect of person, in my heart and go to hell because of it.

This is the kind of God we serve—a God who will let us know what we need to get right and what we need to correct in order to make it to Heaven. God doesn't accept just anything. Jesus Christ is a God of perfection.

Matthew 25:2 states, "Five were wise and five were foolish." Which are you? I hope you look up the history of scripture.

17. ORAL LAW OF THE TALMUDIC QUOTES

I wanted to save this next bit for last so you can look up the oral law of the Pharisees (written laws against women) and learn more.

Talmudic quotes illustrate this.

One Jewish prayer says, "Praise God He hasn't created me a gentile, a woman, or an ignorant man. The woman is in all things inferior to the man."

Only men could speak in public (**Beraktoth 4:36**; **Mishnah Aboth 1:5**). No woman could give a testimony or conduct business (**Mishnah Shabbah 4:1**). Women were viewed with disregard and repression, and the Talmud contains many distasteful insults to women's character. Women were to be avoided. Women were not required to know or fulfill the law, so few were educated in this respect.

One said, "May the words of the Torah be burned rather than be given to a woman in public worship." Women were segregated and silenced, so they had to ask questions of their husbands at home.

Clearly Paul, writer of **1 Corinthians 14:34–35**, went against these Pharisees who used Jewish law to support their views. Paul basically said, "Not in this church, and not in any other church that God has established through me."

The Jewish Women's Archive, particularly the article "Post-Biblical and Rabbinic Women" by Tal IIan, tells us that in Jewish antiquity, women were not viewed as equal to men.

The services that Orthodox Jews hold in their synagogues today separate the men from the women. The service is provided for men only. Women are not encouraged to learn what their husbands learn; they can only watch the service from the gallery, for their place is at home, not with things too high for them. It would be shameful for women to speak publicly.

Jesus let us know that he doesn't tolerate prejudice in any form and that we have to love God enough not to tolerate such actions of any kind in the body of Christ. When we see that the Holy Scriptures are backed up by facts and history, then we should come to our senses. Feeling awful, feeling bad about what we've done, should lead us to repent and ask God to remove from our thinking this wrong teaching. We should ask God to renew our thoughts and give us a hunger to search out the truth of his scriptures so we will not miss Heaven.

Even just the *thought* of missing Heaven is scary to me. Instead, I'm grateful that God has given me such a love of the truth and a desire not to partake of wrong teachings and deeds. I love being a Christian, and I love being able to search the word of God, along with learning about history and language. Before I became a pastor I studied the lessons given by my leader and the doctrine of my church, and then I asked questions to see if my pastor knew the truth. If not, I'd ask them to have a private conversation with me about the doctrine of my church and where that doctrine came from. And if the church was not following the teachings of Jesus Christ and all that Jesus commanded the disciples to do throughout the whole Bible, then I couldn't follow it.

So many religious organizations are divided because the leaders of those organizations are following their organization's teachings when they should be following all the teachings of Jesus Christ.

Ephesians 5:6–7 tells us, "Do not be deceived with empty words, because of such things God's wrath comes on the sons of disobedience. Do not be partakers with them. Walk as children of the light."

This is what I am doing: walking in the light, trying to share this light with those who are still in darkness. I know that not everyone will receive, but those who *will* see and hear belong to God.

Matthew 22:23–32 tells us that the Sadducees did not believe in the Resurrection, so they challenged Jesus with a question about resurrection: A woman had seven husbands, and the law of Moses said that if the husband dies, the brother or next of kin would marry the wife and raise the seed (children). The first through seventh husbands died, leaving no children, and then the woman died. Whose wife would she be in the Resurrection?

Jesus told the Sadducees that they were in error, not understanding the scriptures or the power of God, for people neither marry nor are given in marriage but are like angels in heaven. Jesus said, "Have you not read what was spoken to you by God concerning the Resurrection? I am the God of Abraham, the God of Isaac, the God of Jacob." *He is not the God of the dead but the God of the living.* Here, Jesus let them know that they were blind leaders.

The Holy Bible scrolls, before they were all put together, were written with male-oriented language because the people who wrote the books were from Hebrew- and Arabic-speaking nations. You will see from history that the "five thousand" whom Jesus fed in **Mark 6:30–44** were actually more than five thousand. Women and children were not included in that number. Adding women and children would make that number closer to fifteen or twenty thousand people.

A woman had to be very important to have her name mentioned in the books of the Bible, like Mary, the mother of Jesus; Elizabeth, the mother of John the Baptist; and Junia, the apostle before Paul.

In **Luke 2:36–38**, Anna was a prophetess who stayed in the temple fasting and praying.

In **Luke 13:11–17**, Jesus healed a woman of Abraham on the Sabbath, and the rulers of the synagogue were full of indignation because he had healed on the Sabbath. "Six days you have to work," they told him. In **verses 15–17**, Jesus called them hypocrites, saying, "'Each one of you on the Sabbath looses his ox or donkey from the stall and leads him away to watering. And ought not this woman, being a daughter of Abraham, whom Satan has bound, lo, these eighteen years, be loosed from this bond on the Sabbath day?' When Jesus said these things, all his adversaries were ashamed: and all the people rejoiced for all the glorious things done by him" (**Luke 13:17**).

The reason they were angry that Jesus had healed the woman was because it made them look bad. Jesus Christ is the spirit of truth; God sees all and knows all. He beholds the good and the evil. Jesus mentioned this woman's connection to Abraham because the Pharisees treated women like dogs, but that had to change when Jesus told them who she was connected to. **This makes me want to start dancing from excitement!**

18. WOMEN WHO HELPED PAUL IN HIS MINISTRY

Romans 16:1–2 mentions Phoebe, a deaconess/pastor who watched over the churches for Paul, took messages to the churches, and made sure the business and welfare of the churches were taken care of.

Romans 16:1–2: "I commend unto you Phoebe our sister, which is a servant of the church which is at Cenchrea [the eastern part of Corinth]" (**Acts 18:18**), "That ye receive her in the name of the Lord, as becometh saints, and that ye assist her in whatever business she hath need of you: for she hath been a succourer of many, and myself also." A "succourer" is someone who gives help in time of need.

Romans 16:3–4 talks of Priscilla, an evangelist and pastor who also assisted Paul with the churches. Paul greeted the women pastors of his church, letting the other members of his church know that these women had lain down their lives for their apostle Paul.

Romans 16:3-4: "Greet Priscilla and Aquila, my helpers in Christ Jesus: who have for my life laid down their own necks: unto whom not only I give thanks, but also all the churches of the Gentiles."

Romans 16:6 talks of Mary, a laborer. "Greet Mary, who bestowed much labor on us." "Labor" normally means the work of a deaconess.

Romans 16:7 names Junia as one of the apostles before Paul; Paul spoke highly of her. "Salute Andronicus and Junia, my kinsmen, and my fellow prisoners, who are of note among the apostles, who also were in Christ before me." Andronicus was probably the husband or brother of Junia. Junia was a female apostle.

Romans 16:8 names Amplias as a fellow worker of Paul. "Greet Amplias, my beloved in the Lord." Amplias was a woman we never hear of again.

Romans 16:9: "Salute Urbane, our helper in Christ, and Stachys my beloved." Urbane and Stachys were men whom Paul really loved and respected.

Romans 16:10: "Salute Apelles approved in Christ. Salute them which are of Aristobulus' household."

Romans 16:11: "Salute my kinsman Herodian. Greet those in the Lord who belong to the family of Narcissus."

Romans 16:12: "Salute those workers in the Lord, Tryphaena and Tryphosa [sisters]. Salute the beloved Persis [Persian woman], who has worked hard in the Lord."

Romans 16:13: "Salute Rufus, chosen in the Lord; also his mother, who has been a mother to me as well."

Romans 16:14: "Salute Asyncritus, Phlegon, Hermas [female of Hermes], Patrobas, Hermes [female], and the brethren which are with them."

Romans 16:15: "Salute Philologus, Julia [wife of Philologus], Nereus and his sisters, and Olympas, and all the saints who are with them."

Romans 16:16: "Salute one another with a holy kiss. The churches of Christ salute you."

In **Romans 16:17** Paul wrote, "I beseech you, brethren [no gender], mark them which caused divisions and offenses contrary to the doctrine which ye have learned; and avoid them." In **Romans 16:18** he said, "For they that are such serve not our Lord Jesus Christ, but their own bellies; and by good words and fair speeches derive the hearts of the simple," and in **Romans 16:26**, "But now is made manifest, and by the scriptures of the prophets, according to the commandment of the everlasting God, made known to all nations for the obedience of faith."

I hope you enjoyed reading this, and know that I write this in love, hoping that those who haven't studied or don't know how to study God's word will find this study enlightening and exciting and will learn one more thing to make their path to Heaven clearer. With much love and prayer for all, continue to search out the scriptures with fasting and prayer. Be blessed and remember that you are someone special too, and God did not leave you out. You have work to do for him. Get excited about your God and about being a **witness** for him!

About the Author

Apostle/Prophetess Jennifer Pressley was born in Melbourne, Florida. She has a bachelor's degree in Biblical Theology. She has been a pastor for 23 years and a counselor, evangelist for over 20 years. She has been a spiritual counselor for over 30 years. She trained to be a licensed mortgage broker, a job which she did for 15 years before opening her own business, Generation Mortgage. Apostle Jennifer and her husband Ronnie Pressley are founders of a transitional home to help men from ages 18 and up to regain their sobriety and return to productive lives in society. She has four children and is a grandmother of seven. Apostle Jennifer started ministering the gospel of Jesus Christ at the age of 9 under the apostolic ministry and was faithful and obedient to her leadership for over 17 years until the ministry was moved. She was ordained and has been ministering for more than 40 years. When her leaders left the city, she joined the Church of God in Christ until God commissioned her to pastor at Higher Praise Cathedral, of which she was the founder. The Lord brought out of the fire drug dealers, molesters, crack users, gangs, murderers, homeless people, people who had been written off as "lunatics" with certified papers. They became business owners, home owners, and ministers of the gospel. She is now pastoring in Morristown, TN, for Breath of Life Ministries, which she founded 12 years ago. In this role she has seen God save KKK members, meth users, and many more people in dark places in their lives in her ministry. She is planting the seeds of another church now. Apostle Jennifer has a passion for seeing lives change through Jesus Christ. She is a singer, spiritual counselor, conferences speaker, and much,

much more. Her hobbies are golfing, reading, racing, soft-ball, and enjoying family time. To God be all the glory.